HIGHTOWER

HIGHTOWER

Ibhayu Poetry

Omohan Ebhodaghe

Africa World Press, Inc.

P.O. Box 1892
Trenton, NJ 08607

P.O. Box 48
Asmara, ERITREA

Africa World Press, Inc.

P.O. Box 1892
Trenton, NJ 08607

P.O. Box 48
Asmara, ERITREA

First Printing 2007

Book Design and Illustrations : Nii Okai Djarbeng
Cover Design: Nii Okai Djarbeng

Library of Congress Cataloging-in-Publication Data

Ebhodaghe, Omohan.
Hightower : Ibhayu poetry / by Omohan Ebhodaghe.
p. cm.
ISBN 1-59221-512-2 (hardcover) -- ISBN 1-59221-513-0 (pbk.) I. Title.

PS3605.B56H54 2007
811'.6--dc22

2006035439

DEDICATION

Otekpen Alice EBHODAGHE

ACKNOWLEDGEMENTS

"Our Government Reservation Areas look-alikes" and ***"Beloved"*** were first published by the Guardian Express newspaper, Lagos, 1993; ***"A Song of Patience"*** was first published in the anthology, ***TWENTY NIGERIAN WRITERS: PORTRAITS,*** ANA publications, Lagos, 1993; and, in 1994, the Daily Times of Nigeria, Lagos, published some poems. In 2003, the Nigerian Observer newspaper in Benin city published more poems, including May the 23rd poem entitled, ***"A Letter to you - my niece,"*** and now entitled ***"A Letter to you - my first cousin"*** also.

Contents

A Letter to you - my first cousin

My sweetheart in love, the faith that stays in me is lord,
as our look-alikes human beings
with everlasting life joy could bring.
To you my heart's desires search, surfing after facts,
truths of such as babies do possess as your right,
Omozusi, as my next dear kin,
my own beloved coz look-alike Queen.
Omozusi, as with your innocence I do hug.

Although you came at the wrong time (of that I could praise)
as other spirits who are beings,
beings who are humans as spirit
rocks, do stir my heart core to work: my faculty refreshed.
For the world is but a thorn and you are the flesh,
of a life producing kind as
Ewu avocado pears are.
Thorns that pierce to suck with teeth of fleshy crest shapes.

This olumu is precious, over-refined on cupped palms
of mercies as were the sprinkling
on water as was air spraying,
I sought far beyond those deep soils within a cave
to sow my seeds of life and all their needs I gave,
as mothers' milk do to babies
even as rain clouds gathered as drips
so as to feed and watch my rare plants grow on farms.

Care, my hands of urekhen trimmed and packed guava,
as a cash-yielding gardener could
when talking to that plant of truth
while tackling emotions of age development
whilst growing really succulent to adore tents,
as well as our dearest Creator
the source of eyeballs on earth floors
and with quiet groaning and pleading to Jehovah.

Drink this prayer, entreaty that was so made simple,
so simply done by your pouted lips
of cirrus look-alikes of rubies,
and made of truth, truths to calm, calmness of virtues,
virtuous garden-bed where true love's own truth grew.
Yes, Patience who obeyed herself
and obeyed Jehovah Himself.
Please do not sway in deeds but to honour be faithful,

nor led astray by so-called friends but to them a laugh;
a cheer of the Fez's good care
which harmattan winds do lay bare.
May you crown my heart with rejoicing Otekpen
that your simple deeds may grow meek laurels of men,
as were of the lapis lazuli
of the look-alikes of jazz thrills
of a guitar look-alike quartets of divine chants.

This canary lives free, freedom as the air allows,
such breeze that was of Idunwele's
look-alike of everlasting life.
Upwards yet it flew, in motion still it hovered
as those so-called religious beings
whose hearts' desires equalled clitoris.
Too cruel, this beast named mankind - birds too must be aware.

Its voice of a flute's look-alike rang and filtered
out slowly its own news of an
everlasting life matter:
"Let mankind note that raw strength misused could soon fail,
and a lady's body parts not her moral heart fade."
As road maps of the eyeballs do
flash out Jehovah's assured routes,
let odour from farm works alone not be your light.

Funmi let not beauty puff you high that could sooner crash

as money power people do in banks
nor the surfeit of louder bangs,
for of silence look-alikes there had been no match.
But learn from motherhood respect of the look-alike
dues of fatherhood's own pride
that was Patience's hands of palm wine
taste that homely grew to protect you from gadflies,

whose proboscises were forever scenting to deflower
our neighbourhood sweethearts; also,
as a wrecked peace of mind could know.
Lastly, let deep feelings with contentment display,
obeying Jehovah God whose love myriad array
body parts for not moral parts for,
friends of commerce not prayers curse.
Now I do go, yet wish lord Okonofua your cousin flowers.

Omohan Ebhodaghe

Homecoming

Now matters of life to their destinations do draw near
as look-alike cages to birds receive,
mankind to rooms & a parlour retreat;
as would an Ohue to his home should forever return
with mind on beaten footpaths, groping on things undone;
to phone friends about to loose a name,
for as workers for commerce were famed,
while unfolding yet yearnings of those now here.

Once on a look-alike's sick bed I on the head pry
as jailbirds to other cells stare
as look-alike eyeballs in clinics fair.
But oh what groans look-alike tears, what foam and sweat
with half-breath and seas of look-alike promised changes,
of departing inmates who fret
about incoming neighbourhood wives,
only to turn away when the heart strays off the bites?

But there is, I say, in this home coming a conscience
as computer interactive
programmed to re-sow its captives
where a packed mass as pit latrines to hollowness
must, then, show, whilst for their peace prize to fetch,
an everlasting life seeker,
a look-alike babies' playacts
as a remnant, unknown to men, strives for the home-nest.

Still, could it be a dream when our look-alikes fail to change
from adulterous affairs fun
in parks as toilets of prayer halls,
from leaving for the village streams and the race is over,
as my home life in earth-ash merged with dust as Nova?
What crescent lurked across Jerusalem's
look-alike Rome on to Idunwele,
to roll the tickling clock of everlasting life's shape?

Path to decay

Hear the lutes and throbs of the fertilizer craze
from the look-alike pale West
coming with non-everlasting zest,
sinking free also into their kinsmen's diseased minds:
down the footpaths of more skeletal services bang
labours from their county town shanties
by their brothers as were our chiefs
to drive mad bustling body parts of their charred brains.

Witness our messiah-political party members,
full of look-alike ignorance,
in quantum relative abundance,
hallowed as to heal our so-called brainless mentors:
rattle lord temporal, those newer patterns of your culture
devoid of our look-alike wisdom
drained of Jehovah God's freedom
for sister-purse, brother-gun, folk of rotten udders.

Morbidly equal: look-alike premature, forever foes
measured ungodly, so surely made,
trance tolling look-alikes to reign:
their ruling is, the same life-blood, forever their shame,
doctors' mirrors of free feigned fame of feminine vain.
unfrocked as ever, unreliable
not upturned of look-alike rules,
doting aground her amoral - mankind's western woes.

Here now is the tragic dance of that odious race,
friends to look-alikes strong black Hawks
(death shores of their own viruses,)
prostrated till spine-ridden before God's oracles:
kinsmen ever mingled in everlasting life's foetus
forever lookers-on always hewers
as non-everlasting stone drawers
with slippery limbs thrumming to throttled disgrace.

Omohan Ebhodaghe

A Song for Osonobula

Supplicants we are after Osonobula,
owner of life to give to us,
we of Ewu who sang of cures.
Of Jehovah God of no equal happiness lodge:
Songs, mellifluous, we sing, we your loving creatures,
whom nations came to consecrate
whom ladies bore our family names.
We know your loving kindness of a family life type.

A newer dawn has come, and we are ever grateful,
for seasons of such great harvests prove
a millennium child of dear Ewu,
for we discern your look-alike endless mercies
melt hearts of look-alike stones, breakdown walls of debts
of kingdom call of herbal delights,
of manly works of housewives' pride
rolling backwards on to the seashores of God who RULES.

Our Comforter - for us Jehovah God is the One:
our provider of all escapes
of everlasting life to taste.
We had indeed gained permanent warranty to love,
that made you to become the God who mattered to us.
On Ewu soil as on heaven's
look-alike's heirs of Idunwele's
poetry of life to which the sciences kept chasing around

Reunion

Although the world rides on rough tides
of waves rip-roaring, corals crackling
shipyards rusting, no jobs mounting
so as to forever be groaning under shouts of pains,
of adulterous affairs, we, at peace with ourselves, saved,
from Ewu's son lord Okonofua
on Oraje atoll, on top the Alps,
bathed already with everlasting life water pipes.

Flutes as congas do recall, our great grandfathers repute
as pioneers as over comers
of everlasting life matters
that blossomed forth look-alikes of charms whose secrets
Ewu knew so well, we, our two hearts locked with a key
as ogbolor soup to ema
and Bible to our eyeballs matched
so we are ever faithful, as to be forever simple.

Omohan Ebhodaghe

On a Journey

Listen Abiba, our daughter, to a moral call
of light for virgins of heaven's cheers;
a bead to hedge waists ever chaste,
not allow society to teach you who you are as were
your look-alikes who could no more feed themselves
as to look around but not see
as to eat about but look lean.
Or your look-alikes Abiba who abandoned God

for lips of urban lights as were streetlights of colours
off Jehovah's face and temple
on to state party laps they tumble.
You ran Abiba as truths ran off with you, as birds
of heavenly callings were to gravediggers' wealth.
Even all bus-stops do sell bread
of life; hamburgers we could not beg.
In vain I watched those shoes with dust of red colour

Perhaps for gladness sake, perhaps, joyful daughters of
glitterati schools of nowadays
look-alikes of our masquerades
of Western bloc, perhaps you lost the Creator along
Ewu footpaths of life to humble minds all along.
Perhaps those confetti throwers
threw away God's divine nuptials
that supplied more blessings of stable lives to adore.

Not linesmen of theorem who fumbled with algebra
to frustrate our look-alike wisdom
of kingdom of godly freedom.
Or was it the manner AIDS seem to lick eyeballs dry?
Just when their hospital beds became colour ash
itself in HIV production shifts
and not some farmers left to shift
away those weeds of non-everlasting life crops of bribes?

A song for Eddie.

What man of patience lord Okonofua could be,
as a mortar that received pestles
so he is a stone that could grind pepper smooth.
A lover of peace you always are nonetheless,
as your look-alike rock water is to us no less
the mother who fed you with care,
the legacy of love that you spread.
You cherisher of enduring peace that minds needed.

That is lord Okonofua, Jesus Christ's look-alike
who leads pathways to heavenly
kingdom as he was angel freed
in Ewu city central that is full of square gardens.
Jehovah God's anointed elder over virgins
to follow morals, uphold them
with our heads filled with trades we learned,
as Jehovah God kept us to strengthen our love lives.

We sweeten strain nerves of look-alikes to thwart
festal of bitterness within
discreet slave class of families
and endure all abuses as cruel neglects as wild,
lord Okonofua oh yes respected worldwide
from Idunwele to Goa
back to Ewu from our Gashua,
with smiles of sunlight to humour lord Okonofua.

Omohan Ebhodaghe

A Lamentation for the years ahead

Is this night of long pondering alone? I sighed,
            I soughed aloud as quiet ewes do,
            ikpekpughu to marabou storks wooed.
Or are other future, our nights so? So I shouted.
Strange look-alike beauties also visited our shores
            as comets' light as crescents' crowns
            as life everlasting as Ewu town
and sought to promote our lives earlier atrophied.

Are my society's look-alikes on world road maps?
            As Chernobyl as Atoll, Bikini?
            Bethlehem to our Idunwele inns?
Are we no more suppliers of masterminds only,
that hunted to eat as to raid as to be arid,
            our minds as our houses of worship,
            our law domes, our homes of courtship,
our roots of everlasting life of God's umbrella?

Oh our society of edinokpiawa cries
            of past loathing, of present armours
            by coup plotters of Okonofua's
roles of good conduct not of rot: bitter laments.
I watched their cherished landscapes of flowers bent,
            of winter rot of bomb showers
            not rainforests of Ewu towers
of candour full that carried on as not to expire.

Now gay liberation now libertine of the West
            as clocks in China as sugarcane
            Islands owned by instruments of Cain,
away from spiritual life now of life's slimes,
now uniting now never united where morals were crimes,
            where laughter was a means for crying,
            and commerce the lamp of defrauding
incest-children in cities who preyed on adults' mess.

Oh our nights of daylight look-alikes light did grind,
as moon eclipsed sun to shame leaders
not knowing God's anointed elder.
Yet when these seals of non-everlasting shackles
melt off the eyeballs of their look-alike peoples
who come for our light not their nights,
for alumokhor not apple bites,
yet it might well be that lord Okonofua cried.

A Looking Thought

This observatory look-alike earth of mankind
do often appears on eyeballs
as mirage as babies avouch:
as God bystanders not of humankind's look-alike oafs.
Often in class: life, make-believes, wickedness boast,
as to ruin our earth surfaces spray
their bombs on lands scavengers prey.
To Jehovah God's people: faith as agape binds.

Of human beings' swinging state of foul health that soils
shoes as status on feet disavow
as discreet slave class disallow
so-called heirs of the anointed brother's look-alike might.
For Beelzebub: zealots of labour's look-alikes - a remnant
of human beings who tango over
office power to shame all lovers.
A lone call cried meekly: " Reason, beings of our toil.

By such gift's look-alike of everlasting life matters
of labour lost of life regained
from fiends' wastes, of respect reclaimed. "
We watched also those whose crowns of life we cherished
so dearly who were able to keep them unblemished
as silos to grains, life restored
and Bible to hearts made mature,
not dripping tongues from lips of red martyrs.

This name

Feel that name Okonofua as in the spirit lore
of the look-alikes of forests
that are flashed also in earnest
permeating through look-alike cities of our thoughts:
through my fleshly carved facial looks her eyeballs sought
by a waist of look-alike beads,
crackling harmattan wind as leaves,
echoing her ancient wiles through the village core.

Look how her facial expressions beckon with sly
movements, stalking some feathers first
as her look-alike king-size breasts
beating so slowly so as to catch my eyeballs:
my head of discernment dangles, now full of thoughts
of her supposed look-alike music,
of her look-alike lustful tricks;
oh, you are a gift of some kind, not a curse, you fly!

My surname as look-alike Idunwele wine taste,
sweetens with Jehovah God's sure time
of that so kind ever also refined,
as pure as simple, with everlasting life trophy
unstained: in earnest honest men hunted that wreath
across heads of hearts of minds
over daylight across deep nights,
silence, away from centres of non-enduring mates.

Blessed family name, lover of earth and the skyline.
As serpent wise as Ewu know
yet humble as a look-alike dove,
weaned away from the sights of mud-earth to burnt bricks:
for that surname alone, she painted her boots' strings
a first name of heavenly morals
that loves look-alike auras
of a virtuous mind - Okonofua, not nice waistlines.

Reflections

From ancient of daylight blew the song afresh:
as horn blowers to life admire
as fresco lovers to arts aspire,
as each age borne witness to Jehovah as kind
whose institution of wedlock remained divine
as a vine in Ewu chiefly
to sprout anew those seeds mainly
laid bare by Jehovah God to cater for hearths

wherein fine fruits of homely character were treasures,
as sugarcane as urekhen soup
for carers of family groups.
Trained with time to flush with Jehovah's spirit hands
then trimmed to produce a right attitude with charms,
not trust of overseers who hurt
but the folk who puts faith in handwork
and settle for old age of youthful leisure.

A song of patience

Each day I sing less as more of you, not as aged
heavy mental bandleaders do
nor as televangelists knew,
but as our Town Criers of genius failing in sweet songs,
death cries of lean infants in pangs of remorse
over Europe's homeless populace,
drug culture of America's taste,
braving direly for their brainpower that lacked praises.

If I sing so - as shop ladies of Jehovah wailed
over local government crimes
of grafts made for their policemen,
as women witnessed an only child cracked and roasted
for your own feasts - in whose woeful gaze you dreaded
our intellect except colour
as pieces of white rags equal,
why must I fear to confront your pleasure-mad face?

For how then must this our life full of songs be moaned
or danced to at city halls
to lure those holding man-made whores,
at Salem that wears coasts of sorrows, just modelling
on your lives of adjectives, their works they do learn?
Were they labels of bread only
to disguise as Jehovah's beings?
But, oh, how else can you feel our chanting and drums,

of hopes charred that created pleasureable tensions?
Was it guitar strings to assail
or to soothe body parts gone astray?
Where hamlets turned towns made cities of diadems
of tourists delight as lord Okonofua's adornment
of pearls as Ewu eyeballs,
as centres of rock mass Jesus?
Still, we moan on, knowing that your fate is our song.

Omohan Ebhodaghe

To Sister Charity Mensah

As I do on this moonlight day to recollect such
mirrors in estates of a king
as gifts to a man of esteem
from look-alike ladies of higher virtues so few
to select: now traversing I am, a focal view
to stare about as I could laugh
and hum to bump as to jump harps,
I witnessed those kind acts I felt as I the tot.

The universe delighted as our Mensah did show,
in Idunwele her known place
where clocks chime her lord's loyal traits.
Other folks' beliefs in Jehovah God I know not.
Yet, one so rare, my heart longed to behold to court:
amongst beds of alumokhor
as pigeons of Ewu do flock
with body parts custom dethroned no more to woes.

Your pen and mind so many praises yet unequalled
compared to Jehovah God's people
in character loans not matched too,
as we do share of that innocence of your rank.
Charity of valour let your days remain calm,
as candlelight to lighthouses fair
daylight as look-alike moonlight bear.
Quietness of a look-alike of peace do cure:

of such, Charity my look-alike, your senses I
love as chalks to the chalkboard know
as diamond to Okonofua shone,
as that terracotta round your neck kept me warm,
knowing such everlasting life matters do transform
workers on land as I on air
whose heirs Jehovah God blessed,
which we shared, as were our nightingales look-alikes.

Ask me

Rain to my bare backside does tear with look-alike flames
I could compare with all sunrays
of mushroom clouds of nature made.
The sunlight, oh, his hands of valour were spears hint
of fibres of garri look-alike that pierce my being.
Always I made honey of people
as Ewu folks were to God woo,
the earth, inoculated with everlasting claims

to life do relish in making me so important
not as ostrich on horseback ride
but space probers to Saturn glide.
The world for once asked me whether he was, well, real,
as Love, also, questioned me as to humankind's creed,
of self-pride, yes, of care denied
none of everlasting life divine.
So counterparts demanded to know whether laughter,

observed on party look-alike political posts,
was as honest as votes, counted, appear
on pages of public media
which delighted all; and, I heard solemn voices calling:
"Take me now, take me back, take me oh mankind!"
" As whirlwind to dust do gather
and a cyclone to ships does shatters
so do homes that traded on peoples' ill-wealth," truth spoke.

All about me human beings sighed who also asked,
"When atananfans to ears sweeten,
accordion to stomachs hardens,
will Jehovah God let down rainfalls of abiding joy?
Will it not be snow meant for body parts of whores?
Or games of ayo that could soothe
not chess games made also to fool?
Who but the sunshine of life shall ever accept Christ?"

Omohan Ebhodaghe

Beloved

True love of a family life - is Jehovah God:
as Pluto was faraway from earth
so too the height was to the breadth
of the sunshine that brightened the earth-cot,
tastier than starving human beings look-alike lot,
more than Jupiter king of planets,
far more than the lion king of comets,
tender as the purest water that brought life to Nova.

True love's look-alike could not be better than - Jesus,
as lord Okonofua's look-alike
dawn of further dawn of more life:
Sweeten, an unspoken melody of such songs;
sincere, yes oh yes, a dream full of mellow thoughts,
of fruits of marriages no less
as onojie's rule made God to bless.
Factual, a wet season rose on vegetable top-soil.

True love is - the spirits of holiness as a force
that evaporated black rocks
as though of sand particles pluck.
Steadfast from Jehovah God to man they always go,
Honest, as the nightfall needed the daylight so,
to fertilise heirs of flowers
to bring forth everlasting life
as loyal members of Jehovah God's taskforce.

Thus being bright as a look-alike of Ewu black beans
as sapphire as pebbles inflame
so pounded yam to rice meal display
with such faithful non-comparisons that made mankind
recognise everlasting life matters from death fangs
of AIDS look-alike sufferers
who lost life to adulterers.
Yet thirsty sweet as honest regards to Bin.

Great Heart

Teach my heart of a white pigment to adore one neighbour
from Polska look-alike stiff necks
who seeks with hands of coals to wreck
and pluck down those fruits of such look-alike love-fire:
but, note, that, my spirit is indeed a lone preacher
of a look-alike human values
and Jehovah God's own virtues
which creates Jehovah God's name: fire of labour.

Direct me with zeal for life to wash these black hearts
who joy in such look-alike praises
and do fake look-alike death cases
so as to map, trap, blow, bend, break also my wick:
see the Ladybird who carols, yet sings fairly meekly
with look-alike joyful, sad tears
of a look-alike loving leer
to stir the Bull, also the fool, to break my sunlight.

Still, I am the Idunwele vine, tried wine of life,
of the look-alike greatest one
on a quiet farmland estate grounds,
whom sunshine bathed for harmattan to treasure:
I am that scarce grass rainforests do dress with pleasure,
as comet on Ewu I endured
for hope the look-alike mock odds
with a smile of Jehovah God's pure pebble, the rare bite.

Oh me! Cleaner of look-alike minds so charred - these thorns.
Ignorance? Force me to forget
their blindness, eh, but with no regrets;
make me walk alone to rout all concerned with live coals.
Oh I know what your crude look-alike foot crushes low
but I also do not simply laugh
aloud, I only now crow
and stretch my look-alike temple flesh, their true scorn.

Omohan Ebhodaghe

Our Heritage

Praise to you Ewu rainforests, flourished as reeds, ploughed
on Okonofua's virgin farmland
of members with a family mind
of tender care of gardens tended with love, glued
on to a chase state, smelling of old matters renewed,
to be reborn only as lambs
grazing on green flushed grasses,
from altars to clinics look-alike of brooks' lore.

Such are your works Jehovah God: pied Creator
of all knowledge all to Himself
of mercies He bestowed on childbirths,
fresh evergreen throne where comes mettle fruits,
drained dry as with sieve as to set free from stench views:
of chlamydia look-alike blights
from such tourists of foreign clime.
This refining sunlight, the jewels of us all.

Nature's own Gardener, the ever-meek next in throne
of pathways look-alike black toes
to light up Jehovah's households,
whilst bidding hills flow, making mountains drip sweet wines,
as stream beds look-alike waters, this life - our times.
Oraje look-alike memorial
is not Volta full of Belial.
But no beholding yet, for mankind's wisdom not hope

may ravish, may yet denature; no, not crooked heads
of America's cane growers
but Africa's cassava planters,
who kept lauding Jehovah God, do inherit the world.
Those earth look-alike lovers whose own eyeballs,
of wit to cornea do display
as computers to lens imitate,
were chaste look-alike betrothed ones - owners of earth.

Vision

As
my night
falls and my headrest
is oblivious of day and night's tests,
a call that soothes mortal man is then made
and which tingles dreams and tinkles on timeless to
fade into the realms of reason.
And I think there is no season
but look-alikes as tied
to a cot
of knots:
then the vision,
so soft to the senses it sounds:
a new earth of love divine features,
of flowers, sweet body parts look-alike spirits, this - future!

From me to you - dear son look-alike

Ah-ha, my look-alike childhood of a higher esteem!
The sunshine which shows me as mature,
the rock water that is the cure.
" Baba ma-ma baba," I hear you mention, yes,
with such sweet look-alike gentle type of ceaselessness
of chirping canaries to cows
mooing with eyeballs of desires
as are cascading rush flow splash of the village streams.

But son - dear son listen; in truth, you came this far
as ants could be to a builder's dues
and scorpions to home wreckers would,
even as euglena not from your mother's care.
I know I did pour those other sacred seeds there,
in the manner gardeners serve
as prophets who call out blessings.
Yet who could have placed you as my next heir oh pal?

And how actually Omomo were you at last formed
to grow so, as wonders of hearts
of an everlasting life type?
Or were you transformed by Jehovah's powers?
Those sayings of a bard's vocation son - with our
kola nut eaters - they do woo
as were olumu lovers to Ewu
city who were guardians of our onogie's gongs.

My baby boy hearken properly to this good tidings
                    of a life-sustaining nature,
                    not have a political flavour.
It laid here, this mouth of mine of such look-alike
corridors of power that must rattle, as do kites,
                    as red maize to the mouth chatter
                    and the flutes to the checks bluster
out, even as we chew kola nuts with cheerful tidings.

Still at midnight's sleep, full of calm from God's tower,
                    hints of Jehovah's blessings blossom
                    forth my son's look-alike head, full
of hairs not another's baldhead not full of heirs.
With tender regards I got you off the bed with cares,
                    not as tulip in a Polska loo,
                    but as prayers to the merciful
whom your mother could be, whose palms do mirror power,

your round head, then, nested between the giant ridges of laps
                    not of banana but of Ewu yam seeds,
                    not of apples but of pepper fields.
You cuddled on my chest, letting out slow weak sighs.
Next your look-alike stomach of a ball crushed on mine
                    as cushions were to the buttocks
                    and letters were to the heart core.
It cools it soothes it refreshes fine as crags.

With that moment's touch, you curved afresh as to taunt,
                    and crave as earthworms could to loam,
                    as a prophet to purer language flowed,
so smoothly those bow legs arched perfectly at the knees;
oh what instinct, what mind power, how so cupped to thrill
                    a woman as engulfed kitchen
                    who leapt over cupboards to grip
a husband look-alike of myself on my trunk?

Now on my breasts' hogshead you straightened up those eyeballs
                    as pictures on streambeds reflected
                    and workmen on to rulers contested.
And, exhaling longer first of all, you then surrendered
your whole body parts on to me with no much pride;
                    household dues so new but not cold,
                    not Townspeople's hoaxes now too old.
So son, all about you, I wrapped my arms of a Rose Bowl.

When, next, boy, I asked Betty what we must compare as bees
                    of everlasting life in view,
                    not adulterous affairs news,
as was that daylight that you turned to crawl with haste,
well, here lay gardens full of undiluted soils of tastes
                    to flowers not Valley Prisons,
                    to eagles' eyeballs not to silicon glen.
"Let," said mother, " improve on our spirit seeds,

shading off the look-like roads full of thorns
of no happiness to eardrums
or breasts milk that kept you so strong.
Let us water our endeavour every other hour
solely on heaven's springs of clouds of living waters
which could fall on mouths that aspire
as were eyeballs that sought its fire,
and, wait for ripeness that was the harvest of God."

Within our body parts your urine water dripped
not coconut water to palm victuals
but as palm oil melted in our mouths,
and, so, permeated my whole front body parts deep.
It blew in me a look-alike feeling of succour so deep,
of fatherhood not bachelor,
providers not of false in-laws.
In earnest, my look-alike heart of yours as mine reeled.

Yes, I pushed harder for that parenthood searchlight,
for everlasting life treasures
that inspired no lust for coitus.
Once more true love, Queen Liz said, "Hightower blessing!"
And you bellowed: "bla - bla worship, bla - bla blessings,"
as mother's kiss is father's pride
and schoolboys to their sisters guard,
whilst clapping still with ease your soft arms of delight.

"Good heavens! Let go my kindergarten boy," I spoke aloud.
"Let the Eel not be a pitchfork
nor mankind sidesteps God's own clock."
"Oh such a schoolboy of lord Ogidigan's honour?
Did he not, "Otekpen look-alike howled," improve on your humour
with mercies not mobocracy,
of a duplex that prayers cleansed?
Oh look-alike! Did he slight your manhood oh my lord?"

No, wife of courage: only our baby son could bear
more feelings on me not anger,
that causes my return home each hour,
as fresh dews on hearts linger only as dropped off leaves.
The earth of Ewu taste licked them with so much ease
as farmlands to farmers water,
garri to eba stuff lovers gather.
Such look-alike slowness of the look-alike heirs

of the hen of fortune trailed along only as quick
as tricksters to men's wives do afford
and workplaces to party-goers avoid,
as look-alikes of a tortoise to dogs must they be.
But, then, striding by, chief Cock slowed permanently,
to joy in coitus not move ahead
nor gossip as lawyers do care,
and nodded and went about producing more frolics.

The chicken knew only mother hen's flushed facial
        aspects of family lore not pomp
        that was a lady with no mores,
whilst gallant Cock, a stone throw from his home,
wrestled with zeal in yet another man's doorpost.
        What a look-alike sight that bites
        and might full of empty frights?
Once more, mother asked: " Pray, what must be so crucial

when our look-alike children could say, Never choose
        a football match but a race for life
        nor a harlot's hands but workers' pride,
for I know now more than you old folks ever could? "
Well, human cycle is a circle of bridges to cops
        who chose family lore over dykes
        and everlasting life not a German Eyck,
and walked across life's own footpaths in such small troops.

Now, only some, just the two of us, could untwist
        off party politics not care
        and rush to book clubs not hotels,
not walk through look-alike roads of double lifestyles
of look-alike pathways outside of which could filter
        songs of praises not of bailiffs
        that kept us not astray to the cliffs,
where other people were wilderness' mere polite wishes,

always moving but never on everlasting life's hope
in Idunwele not Ibiza
that focused on buttocks not Jesus.
Alone I watched mankind on look-alike beaten
turnpikes of dried crippled minds in haste so sudden
for the light of Jehovah God
which pulled us up away from rots.
This insight is the truth for mankind, as we know,

that could open eyeballs of look-alike hearts with fresh
plantain leaves of Ewu not Ham
of Vivildi's look-alike hands,
but the virtuous lord Okonofua always with us;
it is the free hours, the sleepless nights whose love-joy
of everlasting life not killjoy or curse
enthrals but no more could destroy.
All they could not beat, never would they court afresh;

It is nature's food of free heartstrings on endless hours -
on whistling palm trees of Ewu,
in pounding mortars, our wives coo.
Now he is life's look-alike of envious laughter
whose senses pull our little human minds when they appear
alright in Jehovah God's eyeballs
as mirrors are to broken bunks,
when we seem protected in holding solely to ours.

With such a tardiness of an automatic kind,
your stomach look-alike heart fire
radiated honour of power
dear son and that raised the head up that poured smile so true,
it was of a sage's healthy look-alike unique view:
a wife's mirth, of a son's comfort,
the joy of householders with work.
Quietly, I cried: it was a life-torch of a lifetime.

For once dear look-alike lad I witnessed peace
in those look-alike hands of wool
of the dye of a dove's plume.
Those brown eyeballs of Ewu look-alike soil types
did flash a look-alike sunlight of an ad infinitum high.
Flakes of saliva by a child
whose goal of an archer's true charge
was all I saw of those checks bubbling with beliefs!

From your gums so real so clean so human I witnessed
your look-alikes lost to snowfall,
another regained by Ewu's rainfall.
Oh Jehovah our God, and tears dropped off my mind!
Oh no baby sons; oh no our baby daughters of might
whom male neophytes never scolded
nor female hookers to them moulded.
Your facial looks of life flashed as if no griminess.

Your forehead tossed sideways on top of my heartbeats
as drumsticks to konga drums steered,
ema to ogbolor had friends faired,
while my breath of vigour could drumbeat louder still to charm.
Still you raised up your head of stardom a second time.
Your chortle was Ewu's laurels
not mushroom clouds on Atoll's morale.
Still you showered a smile of blessings of a column's grit.

You - you did tender lovely son of good fortune
move God to smile, not the skylines
that rumbled with bombs, our by-lines?
Out of Nene's age you made the girl of desires,
even as the Queen tiptoed, even as Eliza aspired
to make me her eardrums
as Jehovah is earth's Sun.
Her facial mien of sweat searched for yours as so true.

Such look-alike bliss of your mother our dear son
does heals a rough spot so often
in workplaces as with households prove;
sunshine bathed us with glories look-alike burning rays,
salty sweat stole off soothing look-alike smiling faces
when a fat lady broke no plates
but a slim woman to mortars hate.
Her buttocks to relationships does put asunder.

As were the victors so her victims' dirge whose scenes
        of whitewood's rot not that of brier,
        from Isles of Blight not that of Wight,
where hairs of adherents, youngsters, were as men's beard
of their parents' well-shaved hairs of unearned riches.
        Whose front seats of non-everlasting life
        pleasure were clothes which held as liars
breasts captive not spirits of true seekers to cleanse.

At long last, dear child, we both inquired what should in fact,
        above cutlass as was under hammer
        not below trust as was beyond rivalry,
be borne in mind as age could force us to listen
to neighbours whom we left behind not those who glanced
        beneath churchgoers who could defer
        as not to be over filmgoers
as facts of life to prepare for when you do incite

songs of coaxing for us after those mental reforms,
        of black & white matchmaking trends
        that bred colour television love sets,
and next to those body parts changes for divine quests?
Well, from that primeval taste of earthen ware spread
        potters' look-alike heart of Ewu
        whose body parts of parents' rules
stored everlasting life's semen as were seeds on farms,

manured by Jehovah's herbage of season's cares
of poverty none of riches won,
of traders blessed of genius born,
in whose birth of labour came forth Humble the first,
novel in itself as the delight of purer crests.
As chameleon's faeces do not live
nor of human beings impious be,
but as potters in earnest search for mates so fresh,

as look-alikes to tease as look-alikes to live for,
as for pleasures not as a curse
for mankind's sciences with no fixed cures,
as love, heavenly look-alike potter-s - not porter's - next of kin.
Shy and simple and pure was her whole facial mien.
Of fame divine not of motor cars'
keys confides, even as chameleon's faecal
directors of non-everlasting life's worth do flaunt.

Love too but entreated of His look-alike God
Jehovah with smiles that do endure
not bought with one stolen honour.
This God's son of virtue, Love, petitioned for a playmate
whose look-alike shall ever speak out with free taste,
not only of money power's aura
but of the sanctity of pioneers.
And so from the airwave came Courage, Lover's own guard.

For in such shyness of eyeballs Courage looked whole,
anointed as were rock waterfalls
to flow on to gardens of lawns.
Yet eager for another new kindred, Prudence - child
of warmth, patience's look-alike rock-mass Christ,
out of Idunwele goes forth
the heart of Ewu that the world courts,
as mankind's agreeable look-alike life goal, also.

Honoured as Love could be but still by mortals unknown,
as garri to cocaine mistook,
as winter was to a rainforest's lore.
It was then for all humankind to learn more of him that
Christ's look-alike beseeched with such command to act,
as violin to a virtuoso's hands
play, so air could to whistling pines
(while Jehovah rejoiced with more simple retorts,)

for that dear help-meet who was half-earth, half-heavens;
of Jehu known of life obeyed,
as Paul to James could Peter be,
as affairs of life to Judge Okonofua's head
was to Love who said, When womankind proved bull-headed,
the sovereign lord Jehovah God's
creation of loyal look-alikes,
as worshippers, so humanity could cry out for justice;

with time, however, shall mankind's pride be frustration!
        Summer melted, winter now could blend,
        the harmattan of life remained.
So we parents, as were our look-alikes' eyeballs
full of laughter, queried: " Let our look-alikes enjoy
        everlasting life of affluence
        with sunlight of no value to men?
A soldier ant bit my right arm of compassion.

In pains I turned to look at the rough spot so red,
        as a wife who burnt a pot could leer
        at the anointed husband not to bless.
But dear son, my hands could touch on your head with a nod
and with such look-alike silent sighing you snored,
        of life divine of tender hold,
        to cure heads not have a cuckold.
The boy of our dreams, what a cheerful lot we needed

whilst not caring about talks of your manhood, eh?
        Of home values not vile neighbours,
        of gastro-acidic cello bluffs?
Yet, dear grown-up scion, a surfeit of your look-alikes
of moral courage with which they could step aside
        from expressways of thorns not of crowns
        of glory bartered for money power gowns
as look-alike gangways of diverse world airs, eh,

had all but led so many to follow after those footpaths
where fart oozes, fresher air disappears,
where haka dance was Zulu spears
on stomachs of the much talked about look-alike footfalls,
oil look-alike gold, of the look-alike man-made gods,
where river was no moonlight games
as glory - to Olympic sports - claims.
Such zest from a lazy world to get all, not tack

on everlasting life pathways that dug on to
fountains of waterfalls not of milk
of crème de la crème gone caustic
with themselves as look-alikes half-truths who never
inquired for REAL journeys' end to seek life to confirm fast,
as bus conductors who guarded tickets
against customers who do dodged fares,
not hide and blame Jehovah their Creator's purpose,

all but all made mankind to become look-alikes
of Adiza and Agama
as were Adamu and Adam,
humankind already involved in the unbroken chains
as errors of non-everlasting life - their pathways.
Not Jehovah God's own designs
but of human beings' own desires.
Now I do provoke those look-alike questions that bite:

but my look-alike son, how peaceful are home truths
of atananfan look-alike quartets
not gunpowder of western sphere?
How so true not to fetch free fruits from Nene?
So look-alike offspring I handed you over to Nene
in Ewu of lord Okonofua,
as look-alike cash crops growers,
as our mothers who knew just how to finally put

your look-alikes on look-alike earth-beds of ancient
lore when times of warmth were due for
sleep that sustained not restrained us.
Our look-alike lads, of this haste's aching aspects
all along were each for our look-alikes to accept
as bamboo compared to timbers
as tenants do to householders,
that we were only being likened to crass tacticians

before being left alone like all pieces of firewood
on playgrounds as were on warehouses
of free spirits in holy houses,
who smeared sacred estates as wet season as with ease,
when gentle fresh air blew out more refined warming breeze
of godly approval not woes,
of future desires not to follow
our unequal folk in life experiences, as suppressed in poised

tunes with a timeless measure of our own pleasures
of gong clashes of flutes that do frill,
of waists rattling of heads swinging?
On and on I wandered by life's look-alike footways:
as to whether it was the man-made all year round race
of empire chase not be God's lamps
in classrooms not on battle lands,
or worst still, whether I was yet the same creature?

From afar the village square gardens of Ewu,
throngs of belly dancers, not of fighters
over love letters, from villas
by monarchs, statesmen and ladies, shrilled out a song
whose firm notes stung look-alike eardrums as they moaned,
of Florentina artefacts in Ewu,
of Idunwele arts in Rome:
"Ooh ooh today, today - ooh tomorrow no more,

if I die today, I shall die no more - no more…."
As body crumbles as spirit departs,
the mortal to the immortal halves.
And so dear anointed lord, those dancers shrilled out after us.
Days will come as past fades, as man's labours drag homewards
millionaires not better pioneers,
of godly names of womankind's sneers,
the entire tolls, all the look-alike stale sweat, mean mores,

mankind's look-alike waiting for the Cock to sprout a tooth
                    of a sanctified brother's palm
                    as the household of Ewuland.
Yet this same circle of life, I never will tell.
Not as look-alike cities of minds as peace laurels,
                    not perfumes of their own victims
                    but noble prizes from non-vanquished teams.
Alas, not mirrors of dreams of everlasting life in view.

Dedication

To Otekpen, greetings my sweetest nene, whose steady
facial grace of motherhood yearnings
were her look-alike rich cooking,
done with ardour that I hope I could now also lift,
and from her whose knowing laugher's fruitage in me fits,
just as kitchen to stomachs be
so our attachment to mother willed,
in whose simple, dearest lifestyle I chose to copy.

For wife, my help-meet, the next to mum of our seeds,
flame's look-alike of man's stature
in God's laws of family values.
From whose eyeballs I could also find true love's heat.
In whose bosom I do rejoice with homely feasts
of love rekindled to endure
everlasting life as with God.
And whose days of triumphal blessedness, our needs.

To our look-alikes, products of our life union,
whose beach look-alike swimsuits shone
with such sunshine where gladness glowed.
Oh! So strong: our seeds whose joyful lifestyles we borne.
For our own saviour, our Jesus, the glorious lord
as in Judah's Bethlehem woo
so Idunwele our Ewu,
whose pure but loyal life no less refreshed his companions.

And Jehovah my Creator, the first God ever
from above heaven's fortress and lights
that must be the sun's look-alike,
from where laws toss me into the footpath He wanted.
Just as the prophets of old spoke to Him who minded,
not mobile phones look-alike agents
but holy spirit lover frequented,
as the chaste, not a cultural attaché, to Jehovah converse.

A Smile for Edes

See such soft dimple smiles all melting off those lips
of chocolate look-alike roasted
yam of no less sweeter a mate
as look-alike smooth spreading of our kerosene
on look-alikes of earth's swampy grounds full of tin.
As calm a cleansing hurricane
to restore hope of enduring fame.
Eh! That godly shy smile, how it flashes with zeal,

as brighter mirrors beneath those styled eyeballs
beaming of lasting life values
to awaken womankind to God's views.
Such look-alike simple smile thus set and is surely caught!
Oh! Oooh my God! Feel those pleasures with full measure!
Such that Ewu palm wine only
could weigh in Labadi as in Takwa Bay!
Oooh me what a look-alike Edes my heart called Beloved!

Oh Edes what a treasured gift from me - your man!
The look-alike lamp stands of God,
for Jehovah's people, I endured.
Oh Jehovah who made the heavens just as earth's
look-alike other planets for beings as gifts of life,
as photocopiers of Ewu
whose earth's surface yielded its fruits,
whose visa on to everlasting life remains!

On The Great Decision

Did those rewards of family gaiety as love,
cascading off the eagle's backside
on Esan Ukato hilltop as
the look-alike Joy glass of Yours, sips through her heart's nest?
Oh did she feels the look-alike fruits of happiness,
no longer of a pizza paste
except as of a suya taste,
with unique look-alike thrills which she truly courts?

Our sovereign lord Jehovah God as you
keep watch over her heart's troubles
from your High Towers of look-alike marbles,
which makes her overcome look-alike faults on your strength,
not her helicopter gunship,
as mouth, incapable of worship,
thus showing my comely consort of your own rules?

But in her life she is yours, who needs a husband,
just as Ewu doves to domes flap
so her alumokhor tongue brags.
Teach her heart, she is weak who needs a bodyguard.
Yet, Jehovah God - as the examiner of kidneys as gourds,
for mercies not of mushroom rain,
of beautiful gardens maintain -
shall surely surrender to me her look-alike hands

whose desire for, Father, is not freedom nor looks,
as seawater showered on to tourists
or body parts only exhibit,
but a look-alike homely love in Jehovah God.
Such is that pot of a lifestyle of no equals on
counterfeit clitoris of trollops,
as vox humana were to disco,
or those double lifestyles of no more priestly values.

Omohan Ebhodaghe

Our Government Reservation Areas Look-alikes

When I lifted up my look-alike drowsy eyeballs
as Ewu eagles perched to rest
up on their mountain top so blest,
to scan about front their God-sent Reservation Areas,
to inspect acres where human existence hails
from Spice land on to their Video land,
from Seafood land to Iceland,
I bawled as eagles do for my look-alike people,

their tourists: these are my real, my true source of cry,
guinea fowls as single mothers
in council flats as Europe prize,
which made me recall as I clawed back my fingernails
that all mankind's look-alike lifestyles do breed trails
of sacrifices of body parts,
of brainpower to set us apart
from standard goals from party conceit from state power.

When I meet these other so-called neighbourhood people
from Oval office to Whitehall
as our Bikini Atoll downfall,
across Government Reservation Area flyovers,
sun cooked - foes to comfort, bridge homes for geniuses -
for so-called Big Apples' dislikes,
their Dallas big D look-alikes
who rhythmically beat on hands their look-alike tools,

some metals of kola nuts look-alike clicking
as to weather the wintertime
as to comfort abdomens with cheap wine
and click further for a companion, I do sob.
When I recall here is a look-alike land of hope,
not of pubs as would our town halls

where lips do trip with white colours,
yet blessed with wealth that made me beat the chest, heaving?

Only look-alike flyover neighbours knew meal vouchers:
on those their Leeds city centres
of card players not much prayers.
As was the leper's aura, humankind passed them by,
my erstwhile noble fellows also could butterfly
on coats borrowed by men on dole,
from ladies on blow-jobs, from goats
coming around their Godless Rotten Areas of butchers,

adoring other look-alike members of profane
outlooks there, not neighbourly types
who held a Bible with such respect,
not accursed human beings from mankind's Jehovah.
When now I observe our mate's so-called friend Geneva
in Soho town of no more hope
in Cape of good hope of no more gold,
from Government Restless Arenas of cocaine,

Ajaokutaing and Abuja-ed from sapped people,
whose flogged body parts are God's sites,
that awaited everlasting life,
I ask furthermore as to why money power Geneva
his overfed, silicon breasts of a laughing villa,
is a clock tower that does harbour
non-everlasting life labours?
Are our look-alike women of Los Angeles -

retailers of God's look-alike Gold dust so fair -
at holidays in Amsterdam,
from Rome through on to Tema
all gone after my look-alike called safele?
None asked questions of everlasting life as yet?

None ashamed so as to escape
from non-everlasting life mates?
When, then, again, I raised up my eyes on the earth,

to stare across look-alike God Rejected Areas
of Brooklyn suburbs of brawlers
not Idunwele land of prayers,
I laughed aloud as to witness trooping so close,
my flyover companions praising the gallows
of cutthroat look-alike Chinatown
in each look-alike faces I found
who kept on shaming their time-honoured virtues, alas!

Take Me

Take me my close neighbourhood people as I am,
same as wells received waters
that fed mankind from all quarters,
making me feel a complete human being as always.
Call my surname as my look-alikes could now say;
not hiss of change but of peace so fair,
with grace as manners not as a leer,
and put your look-alike's householder like mine calm.

Make me feel life in my Ewu hometown of lore,
of riddles care of life to like
not viagra, Western world's rights.
For, Jehovah's kindness, slow to give never demeans.
But gold - that railing - demon look-alike blinded me,
by foreign tourists as scabies,
the look-alikes of dung beetles.
Glamour that class bug in cities hooked me as sores,

and sweet fame that trickster of the West lured us
out of farmlands on to cities
to feed fat cats, lean industries.
Oh accept me, seize my look-alike, tear my pride,
as well as showing roughly all that I used to hide:
of family values to heed,
for a like-minded folk not to weed,
that I might listen to tales of life my love,

be humble with look-alike joy of our baby child,
whom calf look-alikes do smile for
whilst chewing our alumokhor.
Trust me at least for now: I am changed forever
from greed which also held mankind chained as ever,
to the wisdom of endurance
not embers of a youth's embrace
that provoked body parts but dispelled breaths of life.

Omohan Ebhodaghe

A Lifestyle

My breath meekly pursues my look-alike the Christ
in households as in libraries
of noble staff of humble hearts,
my earliest edition Bible of light my torch to walk
that I might humbly read out your work as life's talk.
The candle of my companion
is the look-alike grass Ewu adore.
To the world's standard of debauchery I eyed

as hallmarks of political parties' delights
of insight to bookkeepers' grime,
of office powers full of crimes,
the nowadays look-alike state gangsters they revered.
Our human race to our fall do strike as to compel
us with laws as lies of ourselves
and assisted in building those sheds,
such bright chances not to track me back to everlasting life.

Of Virtue and Look-alike Patience

How can you know, oh, dear look-alike of mine
when on our wife's pillow we meet
to discuss where our affairs could lead,
meditating on sorrows you talk about with tears
so frequently we could also not sleep for years?
Even as potters are to clay mugs
so I tried to rescue you from morgues.
Yet your sorrows have filled my heart these years so fine!

You can know me if we both try to grow,
not as ageing rock stars do foil
but as daffodils grow also on Ewu soil,
sharing together the footpath that I do take.
Can you feel me if I am also in entrails,
alone, at an Ewu rail track
while being fascinated to distract
me away from brooding on those secrets of your own,

so even as look-alikes of cheerfulness to trail,
not aided by your Braille to see
as oriwo soup could yet free
families from such headaches that compounded your days?
You can always know me if ever you do say,
I am ready to produce broods
of ourselves as Jehovah ruled,
just as I am so our look-alikes must remain.

Have you so read me in books after handbooks as wit,
as recital is to holy men,
Okonofua is to urekhen,
so we are whilst turning more pages of hope,
so bright and yet always so lonely to behold,
not as fallen avocado pears
but look-alike of virgin peers
who together have made total human beings to fit?

You can know me better than religious people
if you drop out as commuters
on train services do to computer
programmers from the rots of our earth without doubt.
How must I pour out my discretely discreet slave life accounts
as post office is to lovers,
as phone booth callers are adorers,
knowing people as look-alike objects of values,

thus blazing those crystal clear snows of money power,
of a past north hemisphere story,
not of nowadays African glory
and, yet, that balanced my look-alike faculty?
You can know me if your look-alikes accepted me,
as I have no video Plus to
woo you back to God's holy home,
where lived human beings of good taste on every hour.

Giggle, oh laugh! Oh yes, much cackling of such joyful
ruddiness of the texture of ema,
not mood swingers of Brooklyn sluggards
who completed no works that wrestled in my bowels;
mine is but of patience so sweet so soft as to roar
as lunar prospectors on Mars,
as earth to the heavens rely.
Yes, which towered over pious assembly grounds to view.

You, my look-alike can discern when next to love us,
                to hold on to lord Okonofua
                who holds keys to Ewu High Towers.
Yes, you must excuse my unworldly mien not grumble.
Such is virtuous Okonofua of patience so humble,
                with ejeleghe dance step tunes
                as Bible is also Ewu's dues,
amongst mouths of thirsty mankind in search of God.

Omohan Ebhodaghe

Chastity: to the mother of our look-alike children

A pious lone flower sways her head around in bed so fair,
not as Charles IV also in France
nor Louis XIV of equal elegance,
but on her beauty that shows nature as purer,
not coloured with fantasy: but dreams as curers,
to spirits revived to soil blest,
our efforts to Jehovah our Crest,
to roll and gurgle and gust all worldly trade fairs.

Simple dear have these eyeballs seen you my mistress,
sprawled across a berth, on bed to care
to bunk to await motherhood to cheer.
You amidst riches! Yet scorned your own look-alikes,
robots who ran after Ibhayu motor cars;
as wife with a head as legs do harm,
as a husband who lost his limbs?
Of man has earth drained of that - bone as could be flesh.

But there is a virtue far away: far and chaste,
on look-alike hilltops of honey,
by river-banks of fishes so horny,
far beyond my reach, behind sight, a single flower
not yet pained by sunlight's own look-alike laser
or lacked everlasting sweet streams
whose tastes retain alive my own dreams,
caged by Jehovah God whose feelings to her first

showered to keep her chaste, to preserve her unchanged
as foliage remain as seasons,
as Ivies come only as reasons
to await harmattan of fruitful reunions,
as everlasting life of winds rattling onion
leaves as farmers stood to clap,
as their ufi missed obotor paths.
That, makes of me a dauntless Christian of patience.

Feelings

"I do witness," said our sovereign lord Jehovah God,
"that ants from our paradise,
not look-alike scorpions as lice,
of non-everlasting life matters called a lady,
played Jezebel with her body parts as a charlady
who ruined her gift at a public loo,
not everlasting life in view,
only to beget siblings of no family life worth

from her look-alike twin who ragged himself about
as of rotten ashes of warms
(highest of the high as He warned.)
They are sacrificing themselves for no more gains
if none are not of anointed brothers born to reign
but be arrogant as to lie?
Yet," said Jehovah God who sighed,
"No hard feelings for couples lost to marabouts."

"Yet, also, did I mould human beings so?" asked Jehovah,
"A water boiler who could soil
matrimonial beds with her boils,
a gazelle labelled as just a good friend of villains
who could trade by barter body parts with aliens,
all for look-alike money power,
none for a spiritual calibre,
whilst munching from tables prepared with money so foul?

On these accounts, what further guess, O daughters of
such low values to Jehovah God?
Of interest to maggots and rots?
You made yourself so who ought to forever be disgraced."
Still our sovereign lord Jehovah God did proclaim
so fair from the heavens above,
of angels of light to adore.
"No more war feelings as a being did surprise God!"

"Oh yes, are these my son's former look-alikes,
objects of pleasure on our earth
as lovers of only men in lair,
wilder in deeds, as were those their look-alike words?
I have observed objects called men, a sight in discord,
avoiding God's passports to life
but holding always on to lies
while defiling...oh yes their ladies look-alikes -

womankind made humankind so as to rot as woods - yes,
objects of respect turned around
who could expire of light of sound."
However, Jehovah God, my sovereign God, said again,
"No lost feelings when a family we have gained
for life everlasting they proved
on earth to reside in Ewu
as on stream waters of life shall their names be blest."

The Seer and a Business Monarch: A Confession

PROLOGUE: Full bright seasons come in their time
and changes in their seasons do pass.
To men all mixed sorrows like wine
do pour heavy and gather in mass.
Seasons of nature are so calm
but times and changes do breed harm.

A BUSINESS
MONARCH:
Many a time I do guffaw: this laughter
in me is a cry; I gambolled as the fool.
The world to name not but love shouts,
and I in turn plays the buffoon,
money look-alike witnesses.
Like bees they buzz on my soiled wealth,
none cares a puff of fresh air for my breath,
there is cash flow, there are people
but no peace, no sleep no friends as callers.

THE SEER: Take away air, see man.
Remove the food, view mankind.
Drain away water, feel man

.A BUSINESS
MONARCH:
Many a chance, this abortive
vow, I vowed. This world is a wheel
of defilement and I the chief,
invisible hands do tie me still,
women look-alike witnesses.
This rapacious cycle of sins
could eat us slowly and steadily.
There are ladies, there are lust cum funs
but no birth, just haste, just mourning.

but no birth, just haste, just mourning.

THE SEER: Our foe is real,
our life is false,
our self is fear.

A BUSINESS
MONARCH:
Many a time and a change I lay,
some light to my heart shone serene.
Religion? It scares me away,
it erupts, yes, corrupts my heart's lust as the Oraje stream,
power look-alike witnesses.
This world made me compromise with life:
a life of good, I ever lived with lies.
There is dominion, there is ruling.
And, yet, you see, no time, no changes, but seasons.

THE SEER: To be nice to yourself
is to care for someone:
for freedom is not self-liberation
but a full denial of laziness.
For there is no privilege but a shared life.

References

1 Ibhayu: Ibhayu means that I did not die on page 1.
2 Ewu: Ewu is a town in Nigeria on Page 1 line 15.
3 Urekhen: Urekhen is a vegetable leaf soup on page1 line 25, page 14 line 10.
4 Olumu: Olumu is a pear on page 1 line 17, page 32 line 23.
5 Idun wele: Idun wele is a village in Edo state on page 2 line 18.
6 Ohue: An Ohue is a hunter on page 4 line 4.
7 Osonobula: Osonobula means Jehovah God on page 6 line 1.
8 Okonofua: Okonofua is an Esan name meaning a white child on all pages.
9 Oraje: The Oraje river is in Esanland on page 7 line 7, page 54 line 9.
10 Ema: Ema is pounded yam or prepared yam flour on page 7 line 14.
11 Ogbolor: Ogbolor or ogbono soup is a draw-soup on page 7 line 14.
12 Goa & Gashua: Both place names are in Indian & Nigeria on page 9 lines 22 and 23.
13 An ikpekpughu: this is an owl on page 10 line 3.
14 Edinokpiawa: A forbidden female genitalia on page 10 line 17.
15 Alumokhor: this is a green leaf soup on page 11 line 23.
16 Garri: garri or gari is a cassava staple product on page 17 line 4.
17 Atananfan: this is a guitar look-alike string instrument on page 17 line 26 page 36 line2.
18 Ayo: An ayo is a game of adults on page 17 line 30.
19 Onojie: Onojie or onogie means a king on page 22 line 24.
20 Ewu: Ewu is a town in Edo state on page 19 line 22.
21 Oraje and Volta and Belial: Oraje is a river in Ewu of Edo state in Nigeria & Volta river and dam in Ghana & Belial as demon on page 20 line 23.
22 Omomo: Omomo is a name for a child on page 22 line 17.
23 Nene: Nene is the respectable name for a mother on page 30 line 12, page 36 line 4.
24 Labadi: this is a place in Mali also on page 40 line 15.
25 Takwa Bay: Takwa Bay is a holiday resort in Lagos on page 40 line 15.
26 Ukato: Ukato is a name for a specific bush in Ewu on page 41 line 3.
27 Suya: Suya is a roasted or grilled meat of an Hausa delicacy on page 41 line 7.
28 Ajaokuta & Abuja: Ajaokutaing is used as a verb as in a present tense continuous & Abuja-ed as a verb in a simple past tense on page 43 line 19.
29 Tema: Tema is a city in Ghana on page 43 line 29.
30 Safele: this is a love potion used in West Africa also on page 43 line 30.
31 Oriwo: Oriwo means a bitter leaf or a bitter leaf soup on page 47 line 19.
32 Ema & Ejeleghe: Ema is pounded yam and Ejeleghe is an Esan song & dance musical on page49 line 4.
33 Ibhayu: Ibhayu means I did not die in Esan language & a vehicle with no accident all pages.
34 Ufi: An Ufi on Esan farmlands is a wood & string trap for animals on page 50 line 31.
35 Obotor: An obotor is a rattle snake on page 50 line 31.
36 Marabouts: A marabout is a Muslim medicine man look-alike of an Esan Oboh as a traditional chief priest on page 51 line 16.